I AM HEALED

WALKING IN FAITH

BY

DONALD C. ALSTON JR.

To: Shevez
Thank You
May God continue to
Bless you & Your Family!

Donald Alston Jr
2018

Copyright © 2017 Donald C. Alston Jr.

All rights reserved. No part of this book may be reproduced in any form or by any means, electronic or mechanical, including photocopying, recording, or by any information storage and retrieval system, without written permission from the author. This excludes a reviewer who may quote brief passages in a review.

Unless otherwise noted, all Scripture quotations are from The Holy Bible, King James Version (KJV) and New International Version (NIV)

Cover Concept: Tiffany N. Alston

Cover Design: Brittany J. Jackson

Published by G Publishing, LLC

Library of Congress Control Number:
 2017964715

ISBN: 978-0-9985990-8-3

Printed in the United States of America

TABLE OF CONTENTS

DEDICATION AND ACKNOWLEDGMENTS 5

INTRODUCTION 13

CHAPTER 1: *Look for The Good in Life* ... 17

CHAPTER 2: *Be Careful What You Ask For* 25

CHAPTER 3: *Being in Alignment* 31

CHAPTER 4: *Seasons* 45

CHAPTER 5: *God Gives Us Signs* 55

CHAPTER 6: *The Breaking Point of My Life Style Change* 62

CHAPTER 7: *I Begin to See Life Differently* 79

CHAPTER 8: *Blessings in Disguise* 97

CHAPTER 9: *Being Connected* 114

CHAPTER 10: *Be Who God Created You to Be* 125

CHAPTER 11: *Coping with Regrets* 140

CHAPTER 12: *Being One with God Together* 147

CHAPTER 13: *I AM a Living Testimony*. 159

DEDICATION AND ACKNOWLEDGMENTS

I would like to first thank God for giving me His grace and mercy upon my life. Thank you, God, for giving me another chance to change my mistakes and under-standings of life.

Everything in my life that I have experienced or had an encounter with was needed to make me be the man I AM today. Thank you, God, for your protection and healing over my life.

I would like to dedicate this book to all the men, women, and children of my hometown, Flint, Michigan, who are surviving through the daily struggles of the Flint water crisis. We must have faith that better days will come. Never give up or lose hope.

Everything in this life is temporary. Stay focused on change and be strong-minded throughout the journey, and be appreciative of life itself.

Embrace every moment because the next second, minute or hour is not promised to anyone. Look for all the good during the challenging times. Be grateful, spread love, give good vibes, and release positive energy into the atmosphere regardless of the struggle. Peace and Blessing to you all!

Special thanks go to my parents Donald and Wonda Alston, because if it wasn't for the love that you two shared together there would be no me.

Thank you for never giving up on me during those tough times of life.

Now that I AM a parent of three of my own boys, I understand the feeling of concern and safety for a child.

Thank you for everything you have provided and sacrificed to raise me and my sister to become the man and woman we are today. I love you both from the bottom of my heart and that will never change.

To my sister Nicole Alston-Martin: I love you. I know that you may be older than me but I AM proud of you and the woman you have become. Make each moment count and keep pressing on being an inspiration to your children, family, and the world.

To my niece & nephew - I love you!

I would like to give special thanks to my aunt and uncle Paul and Lenora Whitmore and family. You have always been there for me. Our memories hold a special place in my heart. I love you all so much.

To all the rest of my family and friends: thank you for being part of my life on this journey. I love you and I would like to just say thank you for all your love and support over the years, in the good times and the bad times. It was all part of the journey, and I thank you for loving me back.

Special thanks to my in-laws, Robert II, Jeanette, Robert III, Dorisha and the entire Lenoir family. Thank you all for being so loving, caring, and supportive of me and our family over the years. You have always treated me as one of your own. Thank you, and I love you from the bottom of my heart.

Special thanks to my editor Donna Bosink. I would like to thank you for taking your personal time to make this book come to life. I AM so grateful to have you as part of our lives. You are more than just my editor; you are a great friend with a great spirit. Thank you for sharing this journey with me. May God continue to bless you in a mighty way.

I dedicate this book to my three handsome sons, Christopher, Christian and Cameron. This book is for all of us. Daddy loves you no matter what you choose to do in life. I will always be your father and I will never leave you boys alone as long as I'm living. I love you more than words could express.

I know there are some things you may not comprehend now but I pray that in the future you will have a better understanding of why I was always pushing you to be your best.

Your future depends on your trust in God and the decisions you make in life - remember that.

Last but definitely not least, this book is dedicated to my beautiful wife Tiffany N. Alston. If I could write a million pages, it still wouldn't be enough to tell you how I feel about you. Through everything you have always been 100% loyal to me, and that is so rare. Thank you for sharing this life with me. We have known each other for almost half of our lives and I have no regrets with my decision to have you as my wife.

Our love for one another caused us to create three amazing sons. Thank you for pushing me all the times when I was ready to give up. Thank you for loving me for who I AM. Your love is genuine and you're definitely one of a kind - a true diamond.

I couldn't have written this book without your love and support. You are such an inspiration in my life. Almighty God, thank you for giving my wife such a loving heart because she taught me how to love again.

I would like to thank every human being for taking the time to read my book. I pray for nothing but goodness upon your life, and that this book will guide you to greater things - not material possessions, but happiness, joy and peace. May God bless you all.

Life is what you make it, so make it great!

I pray that whatever you are going through, you will now realize that you're never alone. Always remember to put God first, and everything will fall into place. Peace and blessings to you all and congratulations in advance on your new-found success.

I AM HEALED WAlKING IN FAITH

INTRODUCTION

I AM Donald C. Alston Jr. I AM healed walking in faith. This day and this moment is yours to do whatever you choose. I thank you for choosing to read my book.

My 39 years on this earth are no longer difficult or depressing because I have learned to love and embrace every moment of life. God has already given us everything inside of ourselves to lead and live a happy life. The journey is real and, yes, there is more to life than what the average person knows and understands.

I AM here for a purpose and so are you. Don't be distracted; be still and let God direct your paths. Find peace within yourself regardless of your daily tasks. You have to trust God and know that he will never put more on you than you can bear. Set goals, soar, and you can move mountains.

In the Bible It tells us in Matthew 18:20: For where two or three gather together in my name, there AM I in the midst of them. Yes, as the Word says, weeping may endure for the night, but joy will come in the morning. I've lived it and I've experienced it and I trust God who directs my paths. I AM healed and I AM walking in faith. I AM so grateful to share my experiences with the world.

Prosperity in your life is on the

way. Believe it and you will receive it and remember faith without works is dead. My advice to the world is to love, live, eat healthy, forgive often, smile, and have good thoughts. Always know that there is someone watching you and that your life depends on you and the choices that you make. Just know that you may be the one who may make a difference in someone else's life. Remember you reap what you sow. So create a life of goodness into the world not just for you but for others also.

CHAPTER 1
Look for The Good in Life

In life you have to learn to listen to God and not man, because this life is very mysterious. You really have to be connected to that higher power in order to have a full understanding of this life we live.

As I look back at my past situations, I become more grateful every day that I breathe upon this earth. Thank you, God, for your understanding, and for not giving up on me.

In life you have to be proud of yourself for how far you have come, and never stop pushing to be the best you can be. In this life we all have gifts, but the majority of the world just hasn't tapped into its inner spirit. I have learned to walk by faith and not by sight.

I AM strong, I AM fearless, I AM wise all because I depend on God for my guidance.

When I say I AM strong I don't mean in muscle; I mean in my mind. Our real strength is in how we think. Our reactions can cause us to be weak.

I AM fearless because I know that if anything happens to me I will be in a better place. I AM wise because of everything that I have experienced in life. The God that's within me is in control. I AM one with

God, the creator of heaven and earth, and the reason that I AM still living. I AM not doing this alone; there's a higher power that is connected to us all.

We all live and learn, but there are some people who will never change because their mindset won't. They are living in self-doubt. I personally believe that life is what you make it.

You sometimes have to encourage yourself, and know that no matter what you're going through, remember that God is only using you.

In life you have to learn to not chase people; just be an example, and people will follow you. People will automatically be attracted to you because they want to know what you did to accomplish the great things in your life. All you have to do is work smart and be yourself. The people who belong in your life will come find you and stay. Just be YOU.

Never forget how far you've come. Everything you have gotten through, all the times you have pushed on even when you felt you couldn't. All the mornings you got out of bed no matter how hard it was. All the times you wanted to give up but you got through another day.

God is good. Never forget how much strength you have gained and developed. If you don't go after what you want, you'll never have it. This is why I decided to write this book. If you don't ask for something, the answer is always going to be no. Why? Because you lack FAITH.

If you don't step forward, you will be stuck in the same place in your life and there will be no one to blame but yourself. It's kind of like a car with no motor or wheels, you become stuck in one place. You have to motivate your mind in order to see progress with anything. It all starts in the mind; your body and words are only activated by your thoughts.

I once heard a quote by Oprah Winfrey, "Do what you have to do until you can do what you want to do." (By the way, an awesome quote to live by, Oprah. Love it!) I truly believe that this book will bless someone's life, and maybe one day, you can be a blessing to someone else. Just pay it forward. You may not see it today or tomorrow, but you will look back in a few years, and be very grateful that everything in your past was needed for the moment that you're in today. Just remember: change does not start tomorrow; it starts with the moment that you have now.

Consider this quote by Beau Taplin: "Somebody who betters you, somebody who inspires and encourages you in love and in life, who pushes you towards dreams and goals you'd otherwise ignore, who selflessly sacrifices their time to helping you become a more courageous, well-rounded and happy human being. That's sacred. You hold on to a love like that."

I find that to be a true statement because I experienced that in my own life. I'm pretty sure you have too. If you look back on your life it has happened at least once.

You can't let people scare you. They are human beings just like you. You can't go through life worried about what people think. It's easy to get caught up in that mindset, especially if your whole environment is full of negativity. I used to worry about what people thought, but I finally had to start living for me.

Change starts WITHIN you, whether it's your health, beliefs, friends, clothes, etc. It's your life and you have a choice. Just make sure it's a wise decision.

CHAPTER 2
Be Careful What You Ask For

I was the type of person who would hold on to things too tightly, because I was afraid I would never get anything like it again. Then I began to realize that what you speak into existence will come to light.

I spoke a lot of things into my life. Some things were of no good, but it was a lesson. I remember driving down the street one day, and was saying, "I wish I knew what it was like to work at General Motors." And every day I passed by that plant, I said out loud, "I would love to work there."

A few years later I had given up on those wants and stopped thinking about it and left it all in God's hands.

Then one day I received a call from a family member asking me if I wanted a job there. I was so surprised that I had spoken that into existence, I thought it was unreal. But God heard my prayers.

I was just about to GIVE up, but God SHOWED up.

I have been working there almost 11 years and I have learned so much. I had just gotten fired from my previous job a few days before, my wife and I had found out that we were having our first child, and I was stressed out, trying to figure out how was I going to provide for my family without a job. It caused anger, sadness, and stress in our lives.

I couldn't even sleep at night, I had so much worry on my mind. I was worrying so much that I ended up getting sick. But God showed up right on time. He is an on-time God! I started working there a month after the call. God is so good to me.

I remember another time, when I had fully rededicated my life to God, and accepted my calling into the ministry.

I had been working at my job about 6 years, and one day I found myself sitting in my garage, stressed out about life. I started feeling like I was locked in a box and couldn't escape.

I had been working second shift the whole time. Imagine how that kind of life feels - to be at work your whole day, basically no life at all, at least for someone with a family - every day having to rush through your day before work, taking the kids to school in the morning. Getting off late, getting up early.

It eventually broke me down. It didn't help having all the negativity that was around me at my job and everywhere else.

I just wanted to escape from reality as an adult. So one night I was having me a drink, taking my anger out on the bottle, and a voice spoke to me saying, *It's time.* And in my mind I was like, "For what?"

Then God said, *To accept your calling.*

At first I thought to myself, "AM I drunk?"

Then God responded to me saying, *Stop drinking. That's not going to help you.*

Out of anger, I said, "Well, if you don't want me to drink, then take the taste away."

I didn't get a response after that, so the next day I went back to my usual spot as always, and went to have me a drink. I opened the bottle and took a sip, and it tasted funny. I thought maybe it was an old beer, so I poured it out and got a new one.

The new one tasted the same

way. It tasted awful.

Then I heard a voice speak to me saying, *You asked me to take the taste away.*

I started laughing to myself, and all I could say is, "I hear you, God." So, be careful what you ask for.

CHAPTER 3
Being in Alignment

There's one thing that will never lose value, and that's the connection and the conversation that you have with someone. To me that is priceless.

I have learned to love those who love me and the ones who don't love me. Everybody in this life, whether they admit it or not, wants love.

I guess you might ask the question, "Why love those who don't love you?"

I will tell you why. It is because you get back what you put out into the Universe.

Sometimes we can't choose who we want to be in our lives; you have to let God choose those people who belong. Believe me, you will know who is sincere. If you have good friends or family in your life, appreciate it. And if someone does something nice for you, such as just a phone call, make it a habit to tell people thank you just to express your appreciation, sincerely and without the expectation of anything in return. God will send your blessings to you according to how you bless others with your time, not money.

Thank God for what you have, trust God for what you need.

No matter what you're going

through in your life, you have to remember that the past is your lesson, the present is your gift. The future is your motivation. Set goals for yourself, and move on them while they're fresh and strong in your mind. Don't hesitate, because when you do, someone else will step up and fill the position that God originally planned for you to have. That's why I had to write this book. It was time.

Be careful with whom you share your ideas, because they may try and steal your blessings.

The only way someone can steal your blessings is if you allow them to. I try to only share with those who see the good in me and show it without any type of jealousy. When you find people like that, appreciate them.

It's best to work in silence; that way, the enemy has nothing to attack. Just remember: when you are going through a tough time in your life, try to see the good in the situation you're in. Just know that God sees your struggle, so keep talking to Him and listen for His direction.

There will be so-called friends who will try and give you advice, but you have to be careful with some people because they may give you advice based upon their own experience.

That's not good because a lot of times those people are still bitter about what happened to them in their pasts, so that makes them give bitter advice.

Make sure the person who is giving you advice has Godly advice and not worldly advice, someone that will pray with you with no shame.

I hear a lot of people say that prayer is not real. They say that they pray but their prayers never get answered. Well, I will tell you why.

There is a difference between prayer and meditation. Prayer is when you talk to God and express how you feel.

Meditation is when you sit in a quiet place and listen for God's response, and you will get your answers.

So many people are impatient.

They want instant blessings. They want things to appear on their timing. It CAN happen, if you have trust and faith. Some prayers haven't been answered, because you haven't truly released them into the atmosphere and let them go. Having the faith of a mustard seed is all you really need. We have to claim our blessings and remember that we are what we speak.

As humans we have a bad habit of complaining to God instead of thanking Him for what He has done.

Don't ask God to bless you, if you are not ready for change. If your faith is weak, so will your results be. Sometimes you have to look in the mirror because that's your real competition. The only thing that's holding you back is you. Know your worth. It's not who you are that holds you back. It's who you think you're not. Some people live for others' approval and are not living for their own lives.

Just know that anything that annoys you or tries to distract you is only teaching you patience. Anyone who abandons you is teaching you to appreciate the good people in your life. Just because someone abandons you doesn't mean you're alone. Remember, you still have God. Anything that angers you is teaching you to have compassion for others because you know how it feels.

Anything that has power over

you is teaching you that you have the same power within you. Anything you hate is not always bad; sometimes it's teaching you unconditional love. Anything you fear is teaching you the same thing.

If your faith is strong fear does not exist. As long as you remember that there's a higher power that can solve all things through prayer and meditation, you will have no choice but to be blessed.

I suggest at least 30 minutes a day of meditation to see what God wants you to do in your moments of trials and tribulation.

Anything you can't control is teaching you how to let go. A lot of us have a hard time letting go. I myself had that problem in my life for a while but God spoke to me and said *Peace; be still.* At the time I didn't know what that meant. But what God was saying was, I hear your cry, but you need to sit down and have a quiet moment with Me, so I can share some ways of bettering yourself.

Now I understand that God knows everything you are going through. No matter how bad it seems, just know that God will work it out for the good in you. Be strong and know when enough is enough. Take your stand, speak up and refuse to let others hurt you.

Throughout your lifetime some people will discredit you, disrespect you and treat you poorly for no apparent reason. Why? Because they see the greatness and potential you have that you can't see in yourself. Don't be consumed with trying to change them or win their approval. God will send the right people into your life at the right time. One of the worst things you can do is make space in your heart to hate them, because spirits do exchange. Just say "Lord, thank you for giving me the strength to walk away."

Just remember that no one can argue with silence. You can't control what others think about you, but you can control how you respond. Leave them to their own judgments. People will talk about you no matter what, whether it's good or bad. Let people love you for who you are, and not for who they want you to be. Let them walk away if they choose; they can't harm you either way. It's their understanding that is faulty, not yours.

Everyone is not going to be able to go where you are headed. You have to create a life that feels good on the inside, not one that just looks good on the outside.

Don't be deceived by the looks of a person. There are some very rich or wealthy or beautiful people who are the most dangerous people, because they use their image or looks to get what they want.

Don't be fooled by the way a person looks, dresses, or portrays themselves to be. Some people are wolves in sheep's clothing.

When God decides to bless you, watch out, because people will try and destroy the goodness in you. When God decides to bless you, he will cause situations to come together in your favor, no matter what others try to do.

Stay focused. I know it feels bad when you know that you need to let go of something, but you can't, because you're still waiting for the impossible to happen.

It's hard to walk away from something or someone that you have known or dealt with for a long time. But you have to, in order to move forward into your new blessings.

Either they are with you or against you. Don't worry - time will tell.

Always pray to have eyes that see the best in people.

You are what you attract. Have a heart that forgives the worst, a mind that forgets the bad, and a soul that never loses faith in God. God is the best listener; you don't need to shout nor cry out loud, because God hears even the most silent prayer of a sincere heart.

You have to believe that no matter what you're going through, God is with you.

What a person shows the world is only a piece of who they truly are. Never judge; learn to respect and acknowledge the feelings of another.

Proverbs 3:5-6 tells us to trust in the Lord with all your heart not a piece, but ALL of your heart and lean not unto your own understandings.

Sometimes we make judgments of others and don't truly know what's going on in their lives. Proverbs also says, "In all your ways acknowledge Him, and He shall direct your paths." The people you want the most in your life are sometimes the people you're best without. Until you learn to let go, you'll never understand that there was no point in holding on. Until you learn to let go, you'll never understand that you deserve better.

CHAPTER 4
Seasons

Too often we make the mistake of trying to create a lifetime relationship with a seasonal person. Everyone who comes into your life isn't always meant to stay. Know the signs.

Sometimes you have to let go and learn the lesson. Stop trying to hold on, hoping the mistake will correct itself. You just have to learn to let go and realize that everything isn't meant to be forever.

One of the most difficult tasks is removing someone from your heart. It hurts sometimes but that's life. Someone who is worthy of your love will never put you in a situation where you feel you must sacrifice your dignity, your integrity, or your self-worth to be with that person.

Some people come into your life just to teach you how to let go. Most people mess up something good, by looking for something better, just to end up with something worse.

Isn't it amazing how we ignore the ones who care for us, and care for the ones who ignore us. We love the ones who hurt us, and hurt the ones who love us. Not everyone will have the heart you have.

This life has really been a journey. I have learned so much within the last few years. You really have to be a strong-minded individual to cope with life. It gets hard sometimes to ignore ignorance. There's always that one person that wants to test your faith to see if you are going to revert to your old ways. Don't be distracted by those who are in misery. Stay away from those negative vibes. Let them be who they are. Believe me, they will find someone else to make miserable; just don't let it be you.

Spirits do transfer from one to another, believe it or not. If someone is having a bad day and they take it out on you, most of the time we as humans react and fall right into their trap. Now your day is off track and now you are mad. The next thing you know, you're in angry mode, and guess what happens next? You take your anger and frustration out on someone else and it goes on and on and on to the next.

So be careful how you respond to certain situations. Forget pride and ego. You have a life to live and goals to reach. The enemy knows that. It's just a test, letting you know that you are on your way to greatness.

Just know in your mind that nothing is going to block your blessings; walk away. Even your kids will test you. When we were kids we didn't understand the meaning of life. We just knew what we wanted. With not a real care in the world. We just wanted to have fun. It's not like that with this new generation.

These kids feel like they can do and say whatever they want, with no consequences to what they say or do.

When I was younger you couldn't escape discipline. Some kids got paddled at school, then after school by their parents, family members or neighbors. In today's society it's not allowed. You can barely discipline your kids. People wonder why the world has gotten worse. Parents are being more of a friend instead of being parents to their children and wonder why they have no respect for them. I have three sons that I have to raise in this mixed-up world. It's not easy when they are learning bad habits from television or social media, and the worst to me are video games.

When I was younger I was only allowed to play video games on the weekend and that was only if I did well in school. If I didn't I lost out that week to play. I'm glad that my parents raised me like that because it taught me something important. If you really want something bad enough in life you have to earn it, because it makes you appreciate it more.

There are so many distractions in a kid's life such as bad influences in school - kids that weren't raised well. Kids watch everything, that's why it's so important to be a positive role model. The good thing about having both parents is that it at least gives your child a balance in life and shows them a good example. If you teach your kids about the good and bad it will prepare them for the real world.

Make sure that you give your children a good foundation to stand on.

Just because it may not have been like that for you when you were a child does not mean that your children have to suffer or go through the same things that you may have gone through in your past. I have to remind myself of this all the time - that my past relationships and struggles do not have to be the same way with my children. Parents, please try not to argue or fight in front of your kids because they watch everything we do. They even listen to the words we say to one another. You cannot get mad at your child for foul language if you are using it in front of them yourself, or surrounding them with it. Believe me, they will eventually pick it up.

There's a bible verse, Proverbs 22:6, that says train up a child in the way he should go: and when he is old, he will not depart from it.

That does not mean that when they get older they won't stray, but it will give them guidance and preparation for the world. All I can do is pray for them and with them and make sure that I plant that seed of goodness inside of them. I pray with them so they will continue this habit when they get older. They will know who to call on in the time of need.

If you do that, it not only will help them but it will bring peace and understanding in your life. Not to say it's always going to be happy times, but it will bring peace for those tough times.

As you get older, you start to realize a lot of things that you did not acknowledge when you were younger. People may try and destroy your family life because theirs is unhappy. You may fight with your family. You may witness things that will change you forever. You'll come to realize that everyone has a past.

But then, you'll find your very

own moment where none of that matters. Sometimes you have to sit back and realize that things happen to the people who can handle it and that this is who you are, and that no one should want to change you. You have this one life. How do you want to spend it? Apologizing for things that could have been avoided? Running after people who don't see you as being important to them?

CHAPTER 5
God Gives Us Signs

People say years help you mature, but I feel that we mature with damage. Our situations are what help us to mature into the man or woman that we are today. Some may take years to mature; but when you are in alignment with God it only takes that one situation to understand. I have come to realize that knowledge is power, and power is healing to those of goodness.

It feels good to be a blessing to others and not expect anything back, because you know that God has your back. If a woman or man only loves you when you are doing something for them, they truly don't love you. This is just my perception. I'm not a perfect man myself by a long shot, but these are some things that I have learned and experienced in my 30+ years on this earth.

It's rare nowadays to find good people. Good people to me are kind-hearted, generous, giving, inspiring, and humble. These are the people I want to be around. Know that life is precious and that we are all kingdom builders, even though the world wants us to live in destruction. Just know that you can make a difference.

Your mind is a powerful weapon. Don't just fill it with blanks. Start looking and reading the signs that God shows you. Believe it or not, most of the time they are right in our face everyday. But we as humans are so busy trying to climb to the top that we forget about the ones at the bottom.

I ran into a homeless man one day at a gas station digging through the trash cans. This man was also pushing a shopping cart full of his personal belongings. He was living out of that shopping cart, and had a cardboard box that he carried with him that he considered to be his home.

That hit my heart hard because that was sad to me to see another human being living like that. Usually I don't fall into the scheme of the homeless act but this man looked genuinely homeless; it was no act.

I went into the gas station to pay for my gas. When I came out, I went back to my car and started pumping my gas, and God said, *Go talk to him.* I said to myself, "For what?" God didn't say, "Go give him money." He said, *Go and talk to him now.* I had to be obedient so I approached the man and asked him if he needed some help. He responded, "No! I'm alright."

So to myself I was thinking, "What do you mean you don't need any help?"

Then I asked him, "Well, why are you looking in the trash?" His response was: "Whatever God has for me is in here." Now I'm blown away by his response, because every other homeless person I've run into was unappreciative, very rude or fake.

So I'm like, "God, is that You trying to tell me something?"

Then the man looked at me and said, "I don't need your money. I have everything I need." "I have multiple college degrees." Now I'm really confused. Then he repeated, "I have everything I need. I have clothes on my back, and when I'm hungry God always provides, so what do I need your money for?"

Then he started quoting scriptures out of the bible. The first verse he said to me was Philippians 4:19: "My God will meet all your needs according to the riches of his glory in Christ Jesus." Then he said, "Now tell me again: Why do I need your money?"

Now I'm struck in awe. I didn't know what to say or how to respond. Then he said to me, "There's one famous saying that I live by." I responded, asking "What is it?"

The homeless man answered, "It is easier for a camel to fit through the eye of a needle than for a rich person to enter into the kingdom of heaven." When he said that I didn't understand what that meant; it was my first time hearing that. I was almost in tears, because right before I met him, I was complaining to my wife about not having enough money to do extra things in our life.

Basically, what he was saying was: Be thankful for what you have and be humble.

Listen for the signs. God was teaching me gratitude and humility. That man changed my life. I ended up giving him some money just for blessing me. But he gave me something money cannot buy-- wisdom and knowledge. These two things are more valuable than any material possession. God is good.

CHAPTER 6
The Breaking Point of My Lifestyle Change

I came from a family where blood pressure was hereditary. My mother and father both experienced problems with blood pressure, and in my 20s I experienced high blood pressure myself. I had migraine headaches for ten years. It came from heredity and stress, the way I ate and lack of knowledge.

I was not taking my medication on a daily basis as I should have been. I was only taking it here and there, so that made my blood pressure always high. For years my wife argued and begged me to take my medication that was prescribed to me by my doctor. But I was stubborn, thinking I could fix it on my own. Even my doctor was ready to give up on me. There were times I went for my visits and my doctor told me that I should plan my funeral because it was that bad. I had migraines that were so unbearable that I couldn't even focus on anything.

    I continued trying to live to maintain my day by getting my kids off to school, going to work, doing all my daddy duties and maintaining my marriage. My migraines would fade away for a few days then come right back.

    I knew I wasn't living a healthy

life but I felt I was fine because the migraines had stopped happening. I see now why they say high blood pressure is called a silent killer.

I wasn't me for a long time, because I got so caught up in this world of material possessions that I became unhealthy. I began living life on the edge of a razor blade. I was killing myself eating unhealthy, eating fast food every day, 3-4 times a day, combo meals, not just regular sized but supersized. I ate so much that I became supersized. I became obese. I didn't realize how unhealthy I was eating until I got sick.

One morning I woke up and my vision was so blurry that I thought maybe I was dreaming. Then I realized that my vision was gone.

My wife had to drive me to emergency and they said the vision loss was caused by my blood pressure. I was so scared and mad at the same time, because I thought that I would never see again. The blindness lasted almost three days.

I was admitted to the hospital for five days. When I was lying in that hospital bed I just knew it was over when I had lost my vision. I had given up in my mind. But then I heard a voice say, *Not yet.*

At first I thought I was hearing things. But God spoke again and said, *Peace; be still. I'm not done with you yet.*

Now I'm nervous, like, "What do

you have planned for me with no vision?" Then God said, *You are going to share your story with the world.* Then a few days later my vision started to reappear. And all I could say is, "Thank you, almighty God." God is a true healer. Mind over matter always wins. It's so funny that when you make a decision to look for positivity in every situation, you will create an expectation of greatness and good vibrations. In other words, the more you look for positive aspects in your current situations, the more positive aspects will step forward to reveal themselves to you.

When I was lying in that hospital bed for those five days I wanted to give up, because it was so sad and depressing to hear all those grown people crying in pain. The nurses were in the hallway gossiping and bragging while the patients were crying for help. The nurses kept getting tired of coming to the room as if it wasn't their job.

    I was so thankful that my vision had returned. As I gazed out the window in the hospital I was having regrets over all the things that I could have prevented if I had just listened the first time. I promised myself that if God gave me another chance, I would not go back to that lifestyle I once lived. I was overjoyed because on that fifth day I got to go home.

    The day I arrived home I thought it would be a new beginning.

But the battle was not over. For six days I was in pain; I was so sick from the thoughts of my past and how I could have prevented my situation.

I was feeling down about the test results of my organ functions. The blood pressure issues had affected my kidneys. I was so stressed, but blessed to be alive. I was going to attempt to do better and live a healthier lifestyle, but I couldn't because I was so sick that I couldn't eat or even drink water.

When I got home all I could do is lie down balled up in pain. My stomach was cramping so bad. I began to get so nauseated that I couldn't take my medication and that made my blood pressure go up.

I called my doctor and he suggested that I return to the hospital because I could have a stomach infection. I was stubborn because I didn't want to be back in the hospital after the five days I had already spent there. It had been six days since I had eaten or drunk anything that stayed down. I felt lifeless. I felt like I wasn't the only one suffering. My wife and kids were trying their best to maintain the household while they watched me deteriorate.

I couldn't do anything; it was almost as if I was dead. I felt like the world was going on without me. Finally, on the seventh day, I called my family into my living room. I had a talk with my wife and kids as if I was dying. I told them that I had to return back to the hospital and there may be a chance that I may not come back home. I had to get my thoughts together about what to say to my three young sons. This could possibly be the last time I would talk to them.

So I gave them all a speech about what to do as they all shed tears, including my wife. As I talked to them I had chills of coldness, as if my body was shutting down. When I was saying these things, my wife didn't even want to look me in my face because it reminded her of all the days in the past that she tried to help me and I didn't listen. Even though all of this was going on, my wife still said that God has the final say-so. I wanted to break down but I had to be strong in front of my boys. I couldn't show any weakness. I felt like my soul was leaving my body. I had to dig deep inside. I gave them the talk about if anything happens to me what they would need to do in order to make it in life without me.

On that seventh day I decided I couldn't take the pain anymore and I was experiencing dehydration. I checked myself back into the hospital and ended up in there another five days. I had multiple tests done and found out that my kidney function had gone down. My doctor was correct that I had a stomach infection from my previous hospital visit. The first night back in the hospital I felt like I had never left and this was where I was going to die.

I was so gone in my mind that I couldn't even pray. I felt like God was punishing me. Then a voice spoke to me and said, *I'm not done with you yet.*

I drifted off to sleep until the next morning. When I woke up I heard a familiar voice. I could barely see anything because I was still waking up.

I never really looked to see whose voice it was. God had a special nurse for me; her name was Ursulla Stepney. She was a great friend of mine and a part of my church family.

When I finally realized who it was, I knew right then it was only

God who had answered my prayers.

I was in shock at first, thinking to myself, "How did she become my nurse in this big hospital?"

As I said before, God works in mysterious ways.

Then she looked at me and said, "I hope you don't mind me being your nurse."

At first I was a little nervous because I didn't want anyone that I knew to see me like this. Then I had to realize that it was heaven-sent. Thank you, God, for your servant.

Is it true when they say you are what you eat? My whole life I was told by the elderly that all of these meats and fast food restaurants would kill you if you ate too much of it. But did

I listen?

NO!! I lived my whole life eating fast food every day, even after the elderly used to tell me all the time, that I won't like that type of food anymore once I get older. I didn't understand what that meant at the time but now I know and all I wish I could do is tell them thank you. But now they're gone.

I should have listened earlier. I guess it's true that the older you get the wiser you get.

So, yes, you are what you eat. I went from 280 lbs. to 180 lbs. I lost a total of 100 lbs in less than a year. I feel so much better now that I don't have those burdens on my shoulders anymore.

God has been so good to me!!

Now my diet consists of salads, fruits, vegetables, and every now and then fish, turkey or chicken. I try to stay away from any red meat. Eventually I only want fruits and vegetables, but I know it's a process and a lifestyle.

Slow motion is better than no motion. One step and one day at a time is what I live by, because the next moment or tomorrow is not promised to anyone, and I want to live as long as I can.

I have three very handsome young men following behind me.

I had been off work for close to six months because of my health issues. I took a few days off from writing this book just to clear my mind, because my wife and I were going through some financial issues.

We decided to just meditate, and pray about the situation. We decided that we were not going to worry about our finances. We said we are going to leave it all in God's hands. The next morning my wife came home early and said that we received a blessing of three hundred dollars.

I thought I was dreaming. My wife said that someone called her and said that she had something to give us. I thought it was food or something for the kids but she handed her three one-hundred dollar bills. The person told her that it represented the Father, the Son and the Holy Spirit. The individual stated that God told her to bless us through a dream she had. We had never shared our financial situation with anyone but God.

Now if that doesn't show you how good God is, I don't know what else would make you see. You get back what you put out into the Universe when you know your power and you have faith. On the other hand, the one who was the blesser was fully connected to the Universe, and is God's child also. It's kind of like wireless internet. Let that marinate. God wanted me to share my story with the world, to let you know that pain is temporary; it's just like a storm that passes by and destroys everything in its path. When it's over, yes, there's damage, but eventually things get better after the storm. Of course it takes time to heal, but you have to have a strong connection with the One above in order to heal.

CHAPTER 7
I Begin to See Life Differently

Your mind is a powerful weapon, either for good or for bad. You choose the side you want to live on. That's what your blessings depend on. Life sure does have a way of tricking you sometimes if you are not in alignment. Focus on faith, and believe the unbelievable.

The planet and the earth that we live upon is full of benefits that are beyond our belief. Since I have gotten older I'm starting to live more. I've learned to be free in the spirit, and enjoy the finer things in life like nature, the sky, the clouds, the oceans, the birds, and the bees. We so forget that these things have life also. I have caused a lot of things to happen in my life that I could have prevented if I had only listened the first time when God was trying to tell me.

But as human beings we tend to do things our way instead of God's way, and that's when 9 out of 10 times things don't go as planned. My whole life I had been doing things my way. It never really clicked in my head that the reason things weren't working out was because I wasn't fully connected to God. I believed in God but I didn't have a full relationship with him. I was just living and doing what I wanted to do. I used to hang around guys who didn't have any goals or ambition in life and it brought me down because I didn't know any better. I once was blind, but now I see that you truly are who you surround yourself with. Know your worth.

Sometimes you have to accept the truth and stop wasting time on the wrong people. When you hang around people like that you will never reach your goals in life. This is why you should keep yourself around like-minded people. That's what I do. I hear a lot of people say keep your circle small. But I see differently; I don't want to limit my blessings. There is no limit on who stays in my life as long as we are on the same page. Don't limit your blessings because you didn't relate to someone. Just let that be a lesson and keep it moving. No one can take your blessings away unless you allow them to.

Never let another human being determine your fate or destiny. Your success depends on you and the choices you make. I once had a friend who I grew up with. We hung out every day before and after school. We even used to skip school together. I considered him to be my best friend. But once we got older things started to change. We started having different interests and views of life. Fast forward to our senior year. It was our time to graduate and all we wanted to do was hurry and get out.

I was so tired of going to school that I stopped going. I thought I was ready for the real world. I was ready to make some money. So I started hooking up car stereos to make some extra cash to spend and it became so addicting that I almost didn't graduate.

Now this is for those who can relate. You know that feeling knowing it's your last time in school before you enter the real world. As I said, we had been skipping school, smoking weed and being carefree. I didn't have any idea of what layed ahead of me at that time. I didn't know about the responsibilities of life. All I knew was doing what I wanted to do. Life sure does have a way of waking you up, right before you fall into failure, when you are connected to God.

I remember it was our last marking period in school and I found out that there was a chance that I wouldn't be graduating, so I decided to stop messing around and make up for lost time. I ended up transferring to a new school in order for me to graduate.

I had my teacher give me all the assignments that I had missed and I did them all before graduation. I would come home every day and do at least two classes of work each day I came home, then I would go and make some money.

When it came to graduation day I got to graduate and my friend didn't.

That's when things changed between us because he got mad that he didn't graduate. So we slowly stopped hanging out. I decided it was time for me to grow up because I was in the real world now. We had our differences; he wanted to live a different lifestyle so we split and went our separate ways. When things like that happen you have to let go; don't hold on to what let go of you. Sometimes it's better to just move on instead of being the only one who's willing to fix things. It's not healthy to be around people who don't have mutual feelings for each other.

You deserve to be happy. You deserve to live a life that excites you.

Don't let anyone dampen your

spirit. Just know that if you have to keep asking someone to call you or do a favor and they never return the favor, just know it's ok.

Why? Because they have already shown you who they truly are. It's hard to forgive people sometimes but you have to in order to move forward into your new blessings. Forgiving them is not the hardest part; it's trusting them again. People who are meant to be in your life will always find their way back, especially when they see that you can't be broken. I know that breakups hurt, whether it's your marriage, your family, or a friendship. Losing someone who doesn't respect and appreciate you is actually a gain, not a loss. It might hurt to walk away but that will never compare to the pain of staying. Don't let the fear of being alone keep you in a relationship where you ARE alone. Don't be afraid to start over, because it's a brand new opportunity to rebuild what you truly want in life. Just know that no weapon formed against you shall prosper. God will always make your enemies your footstool.

Relationships cannot grow without the proper amount of communication. A person who truly loves you will never let you go, no matter how hard the situation is. If you're not around someone who wants to bring out the best in you, then that's not God-given. A true relationship is two imperfect people refusing to give up on each other. No matter how much you disagree you will still find a way by the end of the day to think or see the good in that person. Never go to bed without saying sorry if you really love someone. When two souls fall in love, there is nothing that can come between them. As long as it's God-given nothing can block your blessings.

Mark 10:9 tells us, "Therefore what God has joined together let no one separate." If you keep God in your relationships there should be no reason for separation, because it was God-given. If a relationship has to be a secret that means it's not God-given and you shouldn't be in it. When it's God-given, there's nothing to hide.

Have a talk with God, speak good things into your life. Get out of the dark and start living again. I promise, you will feel so much better.

Just start off slow at your own pace. It's crazy to me how some people will sacrifice their families just to say they made it to the top. We go to work most of our days just to survive and maintain lifestyles.

It is sad that close relationships become distant, because our time is tied up in our jobs in order to keep and maintain possessions, and acquire even more.

So it's a never-ending battle. Sometimes you just want to be invisible to the world, live, and escape the place where everybody knows your name. That's why some people change their name; they don't want to be identified with the person they used to be. It's called growth, when you know it's time for your life to go to the next level. Your thoughts are no longer the same, your taste for foods change, the way you see people becomes different. You start to feel alone, like you're all by yourself and you become cautious about everything around you. But your vision is clearer; everything will start to make sense. It's such a great feeling, to be out of bondage. As

I'm writing this I AM just speaking through my heart, mind and soul, letting my fingers explain my thoughts.

Everything that I have told you are the experiences of my life. This is what I see from my perspective. I AM just trying to plant a seed of goodness into the world. This book is not meant to change anyone's thoughts or beliefs but to let you see what it's like to hear what another human being feels as they walk this daily life.

So many people are caught up in racial issues that they forget that we all bleed, breathe, eat, sleep, talk, walk, feel pain, feel the rain, cry, lie, love, hate, have families, have mothers, have fathers, and have life.

After all that being said, some people still hate one another because of the color of our skin. It's a sad world to me. God created us all to be different.

To the one reading this book: You're never too old or too broken to love again. When you wake up and realize who you really are, what is meant for you won't pass by you. May the next few months be a period of beautiful transformation. As you get older you will start to understand more and more that it's not about what you look like or what you own, it's all about the person you've become.

There are four very important

words in life: love, honesty, truth, and respect. Without these in your life, you don't have much. I learned to give not because I have a lot, but because I know exactly how it feels to have nothing.

I will admit, it's hard to help some people because there are so many fraudulent acts out here in the world that it makes it hard to trust. That's when you let God decide who he wants you to bless. I make sure that I never judge people by their past because, just like you, people learn from their mistakes. That's what makes people change. By their past and throughout all of this, people will move on. A good relationship is when someone accepts your past, supports your present, loves you, and encourages your future. We were created to be loved. Material things were created to be used.

The reason the world is in so much chaos is because it's been switched; material things are being loved and people are being used. I watch my sons every day fight and argue over material things. It's sad to see another human being act like that over something that could break, but yet believe it's worth hurting each other for. I look at them and it hurts me to know that I'm the one who gave them those things. I guess I thought that would make them love me more, but it made it worse; now, when we go somewhere, they feel they are going to get something. When they don't, they have a fit. If only I knew some of these things when I was younger. I'm pretty sure you say the same thing sometimes. It's never too late to make a change. We made some major changes in our household with our children. After one month, it's already working. We've begun to see a difference in them. They say follow the leader, so I had to lead. Thank you, God, for your mercy upon me, my family and our loved ones. To whomever is reading this book: I love you and I pray for nothing but goodness upon your life. Say it with me: "I AM healed walking in faith- thank you, God"

"I AM healed walking in faith - thank you, God" "I AM healed walking in faith - thank you, God"

"Thank you!"

Now that we have touched in agreement let our blessings begin!

CHAPTER 8
Blessings in Disguise

I AM. Two of the most powerful words, for what you put after them shapes your reality. I will forever be mindful of what and who I AM allowing into my space. You will know you made the right decision, you will feel stress leaving your body, your mind, and just your life period.

When I AM in full contact with my soul I feel grateful, humble, full of love, full of faith, grounded, relaxed, brave, safe, happy, and I see good in people. I see solutions. I feel I can accomplish almost anything. When I'm not in contact with my soul I feel afraid, empty, worried, irritated, depressed, sad, angry, stressed, shutdown, and I think too much. I see problems, not solutions. One thing I feel you shouldn't try to do is stop everything from happening.

Sometimes you're supposed to feel awkward.

Sometimes it's necessary because it's all part of you getting to that next level of your life.

The longer you have to wait for something, the more you will appreciate it when it finally arrives. The harder you have to fight for something, the more priceless it becomes once you achieve it. Enjoy the journey; all good things are worth waiting for and worth fighting for.

As people we sometimes feel as

if others are imitating what we do. There's no need to get mad. Look at it as being an inspiration. We need to just look deep in our souls and feel joy that we did something so great that we inspired another human being on this earth. Be open-minded and willing to learn from others regardless of someone's race or age. Everyone has something you can learn from them, even if you never have a conversation.

Sometimes it's okay just to observe other peoples' cultures and ways of living. Never judge anyone because there's always a reason people are the way they are.

I signed up for a Dale Carnegie course, and that is when my

breakthrough came. It opened my eyes to a better understanding of life and for the first time I actually felt like I wasn't alone. I learned that other families and people were going through the same things that I was. I wasn't going to take the class at first but I had an awesome co-worker, Lolita Boyce, who recommended that I take the class.

At first I was not interested; I decided to meditate on it and God spoke to me and put it on my heart heavily to take the class, so I did. I will say that it was one of the best gifts someone had given me in a long time. It changed my life. I had an awesome instructor, Sarah Villanueva-Potberry, who was so inspiring that it was contagious. That class made me step out of my comfort zone. From that class I have learned to be more understanding and less judgmental, and how to be supportive of others when they are going through a tough time, because they are trying to survive just like you.

It also helped me to become a better leader. Life is not supposed to be a competition; we should all be able to share our blessings together and be happy for one another. God did not create all of us to be the same. We may have a look-alike or a twin, but even twins are different from each other.

So many people worry about others' gifts that they never take the time to use their own. If you really look at life you will see how many different gifts are being used in the world. You have doctors, lawyers, attorneys, singers, rappers, judges, actors, football players, basketball players, soccer players, baseball players, comedians, and the list goes on and on. Yet the world is steadily in confusion, jealousy, envy, and hatred, all because someone hasn't tapped into his or her own potential. You can be whatever you want in this life. The army teaches you to be all you can be; why not be the best part of you?

There will always be someone who tries to condemn you or down you and tries to discourage you.

Don't listen to the nay-sayers or the doubters. You don't have to prove anything to them; they are human just like you. When you see or meet people with that kind of nature, you have to ignore them and don't be distracted. Protect your spirit from being tainted. Don't give a person power over your spirit, your mind, your emotions or your physical self.

    I used to let the simplest things get to me. Perfect example: my job is a very stressful place. There are several different spirits, beliefs, and races all in one building trying to make a living for themselves. You have the workers and you have management and everyone there is trying to get to the top, out-do one another, or like me, just trying to make it through the day. This can change people's true characters and sometimes they all are against one another instead of working together to meet goals.

Most supervisors are in competition trying to get to a higher level, so they don't always respect the workers. Sometimes management fails to realize that they are workers also. Unless you own your own company, there will always be someone above the next. People who are wealthy, successful or have higher positions in life should never degrade another human being. What some people don't realize is that as quickly as God has blessed you, he can easily reverse it.

Some people don't know how to separate their home life from their work life. You have to be a strong-minded individual to be able to separate the two. If you are not strong enough, your negative energy will be felt by others. There is no need to worry about negative things a person says about you. It's normally a sign that they may be jealous or envious of you. People who were once close sometimes become strangers because of jealousy. This is because they are sometimes not happy with themselves. When that happens it's time to let go and continue to move on and love them from a distance. They have already shown you their true colors.

Another thing that I have noticed is when you finally decide to wash your hands of someone, they always come back as if nothing had ever happened.

Some people don't realize the hurt and pain that they put on others. I'm so glad that I'm connected to God because if I were to treat certain people the way they treated me they probably would really dislike me. I really understand now what that statement means when people say we are born into a world of sin. You really have to be focused in this life and in alignment with God in order to not become like those evildoers. Know who's in control, which is God, and know that everything will fall into place when you realize what you are good at. Whatever you are good at is your gift.

Don't be afraid to fail. You win some and you lose some, but as long as you live to see another day, there's a chance to make it better next time. Keep practicing and studying and watch what happens. Remember to live in the moment, not the past or the future. Don't give up if it doesn't work out the first time. You have to P.U.S.H. (Pray Until Something Happens). Meditate on it; God will provide you with the blueprint to your success if you allow him to.

As I'm writing this now, today has been a blessing! Success, prosperity, and good health have naturally found their way into my life today.

I enjoy watching things manifest throughout my days. It feels even better when I'm able to share these blessings with others. When we are loved well, we heal and grow and so do others.

Therefore we should love without expectations and agendas. Understand that you have to be in alignment in order to experience the awesome feeling that takes over your soul. God didn't put us here to rule over each other; he put us here to love one another. This is why there are so many power struggles in this world - because of so many peoples' egos. This is why you can have two friends and you love them both, and think they are both great people but they won't love each other. This is also why we have so many broken homes and family break-ups. We shouldn't get caught up in our egos. You see, there's a difference when you do things through the goodness of your heart and when you do things through your ego.

God has always brought me through. I'm just happy to be alive. Every day it's a blessing to wake up and walk around with all my limbs on my body. There is someone you may know - or maybe it is you reading this - who may be disabled. If this is you, it's going to be okay. God says it's not over yet. Take the time to share your experience. You never know who you could bless.

I try to study as much as I can and since I have been studying I have found out that there are laws that say karma will come back to you. I AM a living witness; I have experienced this for myself. You get back what you put out. If you put out love, love comes back. If you put out hate, hate will come back to you. It may not come from the same person or come from the same place, but it will come, no matter what.

We are all connected to God in this Universe. Some things we will be amazed by, things that have come into our lives, or things that we have experienced, that we know could only be God who created these laws, and that's why it comes back around. How many times have you thought of someone and they were in your spirit or you were just reflecting on a memory and then an hour or day or month passes by and you see them and they say they were thinking of you also? That is because we are all connected.

My wife and I were talking one day about a family member that we haven't seen in a while. That SAME DAY we ran into them, though it had been years since we had seen them. That's nothing but God; we spoke it into existence. It is strange how we get the most love from people who barely know us, who go off first impressions, who don't know anything about our upbringing. But sometimes once we get to know each other this changes.

There was a time when blood was thicker than water. Now we are living in times where children don't speak to their parents and siblings don't speak to one another because of jealousy or because they just don't relate. As a new generation of parents and grandparents, we need to instill in our children minds to love one another unconditionally, whether wrong or right. We have to be the bigger person sometimes and lift them up and let them know it's going to be alright and that they will never be alone.

Have you noticed that all the

blessed ones are the ones who give and love unconditionally? Several times in life you may go out of your way to do a good deed for someone who doesn't appreciate it. Try not to focus on their lack of appreciation. Remember that what you have done is between you and God, not you and the individual.

CHAPTER 9
Being Connected

If you look at my book cover you will see the symbolization of me starting at the bottom and staying in the center where the heart is love. I know that when you go to the top it's a cold and lonely place, and I always want to love because that's what God created us to do.

The frog on the front cover represents the seven days of transformation as I wrote this book. A tree frog sat at my windowsill for seven days; he left the house every night at the same time and came back every morning at the same time.

He was there for hours during the day. I could open and close the window. I could touch the screen. I even talked to him and he did not move. I never touched him, even though I could have, because I knew his purpose for being there.

I was so in alignment and connected to God that I knew the feeling of peace this frog gave me was spiritual. So I did my research: The spiritual meaning of this frog is transformation, detox, lifestyle changes, and cleansing.

On that 7th day of writing this book I felt a sensation that came over my body and heart and I knew my book was complete.

My wife came home from work and instantly looked out the window, which she had been doing every day, and she said, "Where is our spiritual animal?"

I said, "It's gone; he left." Then I thought about it and I said, "I know why he left."

When my wife asked why, I said, "Because I finished my book."

He was only temporary, just like the other things in our life that are temporary. But if you allow God to be in your heart you will receive everything he puts in your life to bring you peace.

You are starting to understand, aren't you? That the whole world is inside you, in your thoughts and in your heart. That to be able to find peace, you must first be at peace with yourself. I have realized that no matter what you have or possess, it doesn't matter. I realized that real happiness isn't something materialistic or food. It could be a smile from someone; the love that someone shares; having a meal with someone.

One of the most important things we are given is time. There's only so much time that we have in this life; live as wisely as possible. Sometimes it takes years to get that one year that will change your life. The older you get the more you will understand that it's not all about how you look, what you like, or what you own. It's all about the person that God helped you to become and created you to be right now.

We as humans need to start helping each other grow instead of destroying each other. Don't you realize that your life can change in the blink of an eye? Look at all the hurricanes that come every year.

Do you think that hurricanes or tornadoes care about what race you are or how much money you have? Think about it! God will wipe away everything that you thought was important and make you depend on what really matters, and that's love.

The world is so full of hate, envy, lust, and destruction that human life doesn't know how to treat one another as human beings. Just know that God will show you what matters eventually in your lifetime.

Be humble. God will bless you if you're thankful for life alone.

Whether intentionally or unintentionally, human beings can still taint other human beings.

We can be so caught up in the wrong things that it's hard for anybody to really progress in today's society, because there's always tit for tat.

This world has been living in karma for centuries. My question is: When is it going to stop? When are you going to realize that what you put out into the Universe will always come back just like a boomerang. Pay attention to the signs that God gives you. They are connected to the paths you travel, and your purpose in life.

Just know that no matter what we go through in this life as human beings, nothing ahead of you is bigger or stronger than the power of God behind you.

Right now you are reading this book, and right now you are re-evaluating your life for new beginnings, and, yes, the thoughts that you have right now about the things that you want to accomplish. Don't procrastinate; do it today. Don't fear what could go wrong; instead, have the faith of a mustard seed. The Bible tells us in Isaiah 41:10: So do not fear, for I AM with you; do not be dismayed, for I Am your God. I will strengthen you and help you; I will uphold you with my righteous right hand. That means no matter what you come against, there's a higher power that has your back.

Understand that we don't need to worry about anything when we are in alignment with God, because he will supply our every need. If one door closes we must believe and know that he will open up another. Don't get discouraged, because more than likely at a later date you will be grateful that things didn't work out the way you once wanted them to. Appreciate the disappointments because as time passes we will understand they were for our good. Not everything in life is permanent.

Sometimes people come into

your life to show you what is right and what is wrong.

Once again we live and we learn. It shows you who you can be, and teaches you to love yourself because let's just face it if you can't love yourself how can you love anyone else? And if you don't have a love for God, then how can you have a positive outlook on life?

Not everyone is going to stay in your life forever; we will still have to keep moving on. Just thank them for what they've given you, whether good or bad, friend or family. Life is a learning process. That's why you have to appreciate every moment you have. If you have a husband or wife that God blessed you with, make it work for the good. Don't give up on each other; pray together. The same applies to your children.

I know it's not easy having or raising a family. I AM married with three sons and I will admit that it is hard, knowing that I have these responsibilities. I created them, and I will do anything for them because it was God who gave me these blessings. To all the men and women who are not doing their part, it's time to stand up and be a better example to your kids, and stay involved in their lives.

Perhaps as a kid you felt that your parents didn't spend enough time with you, or you didn't have your parents in your life. It may have hurt during those years, but look at you now. You made it this far and you are still standing.

God works in mysterious ways; he is faithful, trustworthy, and dependable. God always comes at the right time. Stop giving up so easily, and know that you are never alone. I know for a fact that God is always present in the time of need. Thank you, God.

CHAPTER 10
Be Who God Created You to Be

As I walk this Earth each day I begin to realize and fully understand my purpose. Everyone on this earth has a gift. Some use their gifts, and there are some who don't know what gift they have inside. It's funny how it usually takes someone else to point out your gift. Most of my life people would tell me that I had a gift in speaking to others but I didn't consider that a gift. I just thought that it was normal conversation but then more and more people would ask me if I was a preacher because of the advice I would give them. I used to look at life through the physical form but now I live through the spirit. I had to let God be my tour guide through this life I'm living now. I'm just a vessel who's trying to plant a seed of goodness into the atmosphere.

When you become one with God you begin to notice things such as people treating you differently. Their conversations are not the same; they keep their conversations short because they really don't know how to react to you. God will send the right people into your life when you are in alignment with Him.

When you and someone are not on the same page of conversation, beliefs, or just don't relate they begin to separate themselves from you. It is not because they don't care for you; most of the time it is because you just don't relate to them and now you have grown past them. The things you once cared about no longer interest you. You see, people are always cheering for you as long as you're not passing them. They begin to see your strength and your potential to be something powerful and that's when it becomes obvious to you:

THEY DON'T HAVE A FULL UNDERSTANDING OF HAVING A RELATIONSHIP WITH GOD.

Never get upset; feel honored, and pray that one day they will be where you are spiritually and also have a strong relationship with God.

Someone asked me one day, "Why are you always smiling?" and I responded, "What's wrong with smiling?" He just looked at me as if I had done something wrong. Then I realized maybe he was just having a bad day.

Sometimes people envy your happiness. They want that same happiness in their own lives. Some people won't like you, but they will still find a way and the time to watch everything you do. Then they feel guilty because they begin to realize you were a good person just going through something and made it out. Instead of being happy for you, they become envious of you.

God will make your enemy your footstool. That's how God works. I make sure that I AM as humble as possible. I don't give any reason for anyone to dislike me, but somehow some people create their own little drama out of jealousy. People who repeatedly attack your confidence and self-esteem are quite aware of your potential, even if you are not. Some people will only hate you because of the way other people love you. You see, how I look at life now is when you are truly at peace and in touch with your inner spirit; nothing anyone says or does will bother you and no negativity can touch you. Some people don't know how many nights you prayed and meditated on the things that God has blessed you with. No one truly knows the sacrifices you made to become the successful person you are today; all of those sleepless nights, worrying about how you were going to pay your bills; how you were going to move out of your bad neighborhood. No one truly knows your struggles unless you told them or they lived them with you. Today I'm thankful and grateful for every blessing and person that God has put into my life. It all has been a lesson and a blessing.

    I'm at the point in my life, where I don't care about losing friendships or relationships. People come and go;

that's just life. We never need to chase anyone or beg anyone for their time, their friendship, or their loyalty.

Sometimes the people you want in your life or as part of your story are only meant to be a chapter in your book. They are seasonal people. God will surround us with the right people at the right time.

Fear will block your blessings. Fear will keep you from unlocking your true gifts that God has put inside you. There is a great feeling that comes on the other side of fear.

I remember a time in my life when I used to be afraid to eat in public in front of people. I used to be uncomfortable about my weight. My wife would get mad at me because we couldn't go to nice restaurants without me giving her a hassle. I don't know why I was like that. I had a phobia of being in crowded areas. I was insecure in myself and it held me back from a lot of my blessings.

So one day I looked in the mirror and I told myself that I wasn't going to live like that anymore. A lot of people didn't know that about me, that I was shy in my younger days. I used to be scared to talk to girls and was afraid to speak in front of others. Once I told myself that I wasn't going to be that way or live like that anymore things started to turn around for me. Once I did that I started feeling more and more comfortable about myself. My self-esteem was boosted. You see, fear will block you from a lot of great things. When you start to realize that you are part of this world like everyone else, you begin to flourish and receive more blessings into your life.

I have realized that my past was needed in order for me to be where I AM today. I just thank God that he saved me from the dark moments of my life and that I was able to live through all my pains, insecurities and struggles and I AM able to share these walks of life with you. Life is a journey; live for the moment and know that everything in your past was needed in order for you to be the awesome person you are today. It may seem like you don't have everything you want but thank God that you have everything you need to survive. When you see others being blessed, try not to get upset with people or situations, because both are powerless without your reaction.

If you ever have a feeling of jealousy or envy in you, just try to remember this scripture, Psalm 51:10: Create in me a clean heart, O God, and put a new and right spirit within me.

Sometimes it's good for us to go through hard times; hard times are often blessings in disguise. I know it may not seem like it at the time but you have to let go and let life strengthen you. No matter how much it hurts, hold your head up and keep pushing. This is important to remember when you're having a rough day, a bad month, or a rough year. Truth be told, sometimes the hardest lessons to learn are the ones your spirit needs most.

Your past was never a mistake. So take all the crazy experiences and lessons and place them in a box and leave them in the past, because you are no longer living there. Sometimes you have to sit still and listen to what God has to say. I know it's hard to forget someone who gave you so much to remember, whether it was good or bad, but you have to learn to forgive and leave it all in the past.

God is good, and he is still working. When you feel lost and directionless, when you have nothing but questions with no answers in sight, just know that he's still working. When you have not a clue if life will ever get back to good again, he's still working. Just be ready when God decides to bless you because God is going to send you to places that you may not feel that you are qualified to go. Know that God doesn't call the qualified. He qualifies the called. Stop placing limits on what God can do in your life, because God can instantly change everything around for you. God will never leave you hanging as long as you put God first in everything you do. You may not know it but God is with you in all that you do. In the Bible Genesis 21:22 tells us that the kingdom of God is within us.

Distractions can block your blessings. That's why I try to remember Psalms 16:8 when certain things try to block my blessings. Psalms 16:8 says "I keep my eyes always on the Lord; with Him at my right hand I will not be shaken."

I will admit that it is hard to live by that sometimes, especially when attacks happen unexpectedly. Our own flaws can distract us from keeping our eyes on God. If we think too much about what is wrong with us, we will forget what God can do through us. If we look too much at what we lack, we will forget to be thankful for what we have. Just know that when the enemy cannot destroy you, his job is to DISTRACT you. Don't be distracted by those who are not like-minded. There are so many things that can distract us from our blessings, such as the media, be careful what you feed your mind; some things are just not that important to be entertaining.

You have to find balance in your life or you will lose yourself. It's ok to work hard but don't let work overpower your life. Life is too short to not enjoy it. Know who you are and that you are worthy of reaching your dreams, and that it is never too late to start creating that life you have always hoped for. Do not compare yourself to others; we are not the same. No two souls are the same. Leave it all in God's hands. I know it's hard to do sometimes but it will be worth it. It's like a boat trying to move with the anchor down. You have to embrace change and embrace life.

CHAPTER 11
Coping with Regrets

Regrets will make you have a miserable life. That's the same thing as living in the past. Never regret anything that has happened in your life; it can't be reversed. If it could, I would have changed a whole lot of things in my life but sometimes you have to face reality and face the music and know that it was just a lesson and keep on moving. I know it's hard sometimes to move on but it's just part of life.

What I have experienced in my own life is that in the end, I regretted that I had missed out on a whole lot of opportunities because of lack of confidence. I felt that if I had the knowledge and understanding of how things worked a long time ago I could be a lot further in my life. I know there has to be at least one person in the world who feels what I am saying.

There are so many different things that can cause regrets in our lives such as relationships that we were afraid to have. Then you see that person with someone else and they look like they're happy and in your mind you say to yourself: I messed up; I wish I could have made it work. Another regret is a decision that we waited too long to make. It could be a job that you didn't take because of your pride and you see someone else prosper from that same job that you thought you were too good for. What a lot of people don't realize is that we block our own blessings and don't even realize it. I have done it many times in my life with many different situations. Some people regret having kids, but didn't have any regrets when they were having sex. It never crossed their minds that if they don't use contraception they could possibly have a child. One decision that is not well-thought-out can change your whole life. It's pretty scary when you realize that you had big plans, and now you can't live the life you wanted because you made that mistake.

Regret of that mistake will turn into misery after awhile if you don't learn to move on and just take it as a lesson.

Some people cannot love because they are stuck in the past. Just know that no matter how long you have traveled in the wrong direction it does not mean that you cannot turn around.

Change can either happen right away or it may take a little time. Leave it all in God's hands. God has never failed me yet, even though I have failed him many times in my life.

I have noticed that the more you try to control something the more it controls you. Free yourself and let things take their own natural course. Many times we try to do things on our own and then realize that it wasn't meant to be. Instead of letting God lead our way we do the total opposite. You'll drive yourself crazy trying to control something that isn't yours to control. God is in control of my life.

Guilt is one of the most depressing feelings to me because, like regret, it can take away from being able to move forward into new beginnings and new blessings. If God can forgive you why can't you forgive yourself? The answer comes in these three words: Lack of Faith. I once heard KRS ONE say that the meaning of "Guilty" is Giving Up Inspirational

Living Towards Yourself. That's some pretty deep thinking but honestly true. God is truly amazing. He can change situations in your life when you pray, and through meditation. I have truly realized that there is power within us all. You just have to know how to tap into your inner spirit. Every day that we walk upon this earth life presents us with challenges. You just have to be in full alignment with God in order to see any progress. Don't let others' opinions or interactions affect your growth with God. Many people won't understand your journey until it comes to pass. They are living in the past and can't relate or live in the present moment, because their mindset is stalled in the same place.

They are moving physically but not mentally. It's time to wake up.

CHAPTER 12
Being One with God Together

Before getting married you first should make sure that your relationship is God-given, and that you are getting married for the right reasons. Don't get married because a man or woman has a lot of money or worldly possessions.

Those possessions come and go but true love never fades. Before my wife and I got married we made sure that we built a foundation of friendship first. We went through joys and adversity in our marriage, as any relationship does. We had a period in our life where we had stopped praying together, but what we didn't realize is that it left an opening for negativity to creep in on us. You have to keep God at the head of your marriage in order for it to truly work.

One important thing that I have learned is that when you know your relationship is God-given you have to fight for each other and not against each other. Forgive each other and never go to bed angry; don't leave each other feeling unloved or unwanted. If you really have true love for that person you will make sure you both apologize. When you are in a relationship or marriage you cannot put others before your mate and children. If you put your spouse second, after God, your relationship or marriage will last your lifetime. I know in a relationship or marriage we may have differences, but don't let your ego or pride ruin your relationship. You have to remember it's a reason why opposites attract. The greatness of opposites is that you both can learn something from one another. Tiffany and I are different in a lot of ways but we both are willing to learn from each other and that's what makes a marriage strong.

You cannot be selfish in your ways, thinking that because you are a man or woman you should be in control of everything. In a marriage you have to balance one another.

Find each of your strengths in all areas. Be willing to trust, listen, learn, encourage, communicate, work together and build. Marriage is about being one together and that's what makes you a power couple. If you truly want your marriage to last a lifetime, you have to give it the attention and effort that it deserves.

If you are married and have kids you cannot let them break your bond with one another. Your kids are going to grow up one day and move out. Kids can and will destroy your marriage if you allow them to. It takes a lot to raise a family; it's not easy when you have many different personalities in one home. As parents we have to be of one accord and touch in agreement that what one says goes. It cannot be you saying yes and the other saying no to your children because they will know which parent will give them their way and that can cause a lot of confusion and arguments between spouses. Kids will play one parent against the other; but before those kids came into your lives there was some reason you were happy with each other.

Don't let your kids ruin what God has joined together. I know it's hard being a wife or husband with all of these differences plus going to work every day and kids getting on your nerves. But one day they are going to grow up and get older, and you're going to look around and it's going to be only you and your spouse.

If you have differences try not to be disrespectful to each other. Do not degrade each other in front of your kids because they will grow up being disrespectful the same way. Be careful what you say; words can and will affect someone's heart and soul, whether you know it or not. Sometimes in a marriage you have to lose an argument in order to keep your spouse. Don't say words to each other that you will regret in the future.

A good marriage requires you to trust one another, forgive and forget, and be loyal to each other no matter what. When you are having problems or disagreements, don't spread your business to others outside your marriage. I watch a lot of people go on social media, exposing their issues to the world. That's not cool at all.

If you truly love someone, that should never happen because interference from other people - and that includes family - can make your situation worse. You should never do that because it can cause you to lose respect and trust for each other.

A marriage is like a car. You have to do the maintenance on it in order to keep it going. If you don't get an oil change on your car what happens? The engine will lock up. Don't let your relationship or marriage lock up. Pray together when these situations occur. Believe me, God will work it all out for your good if you allow him to. Go to God first. You have to trust God, not people, and you have to depend on God and not your own ways.

It's all because of God's grace that he has allowed my marriage to be restored and remain strong. Marriage is hard work but it's not a job when it's real love.

A good marriage requires time, effort, molding, and lots of praying together. It's a connection and a commitment. The world that we live in today makes it so hard to maintain a strong marriage because of distractions and temptations. Our lives are so busy with our children, employment, daily activities, and other challenges, which can cause us to look at our spouses as business partners. I've been married almost 13 years and the love is still there because we both choose to forgive often and love one another unconditionally.

Some people may get tired of being married to the same person and feel stuck in the same routine. Once your mind matures, though, you begin to realize that every day you live, you and your spouse are different.

Every experience you have in life creates a new you. Therefore I'm not the same man that my wife Tiffany married 13 years ago and neither is she the same woman. After 5 years of marriage and my first child I begin to notice that love was fading away in my marriage. This was because we were putting our time and effort into everything else, and giving crumbs to one another.

I didn't want my marriage to fail so we made some changes because things were falling apart. The first change was knowing and understanding that we are good at whatever we focus on and put our minds to. So I began to focus not on my wife but on my relationship with God.

Marriage has to be based on love and many other things. If there is no love in your relationship there is no need to be married.

Marriage is about being one together. Prior to marriage, all of your personal desires have to be fulfilled before becoming a family; if not, you will not be satisfied with your decision. When I decided to get married I was fully ready because she was my friend first.

When I met Tiffany I knew one day that she would be my wife. I actually told her this the first day we met. It took me years to realize and understand that my wife and I were one together. As we became spiritually stronger together our minds were no longer focused on material possessions or our own egos. We began to be more focused and concerned the most with our relationship with God and one another. We knew that no matter what we went through there was a Higher Power that could intervene as long as we had Faith. Our trust is fully in God and not one another because we are both humans. This is what allows us to forgive each other and continue to love one another without any separation. I AM proud to say that my wife is my best friend because we do almost everything together. Our marriage is not 50/50; it's 100% togetherness. We are one, and no weapon formed against us shall prosper. Marital knowledge is strength, and prosperity is within both of you!

CHAPTER 13
I AM A Living Testimony

I thank God for giving me another chance to make lifestyle changes. I spent almost my whole life living with bad habits and the results of that caused me to live an unhealthy life not just physically, but mentally also. I never took the time to think of the future. My way of thinking has changed along with the way I choose to eat.

As I mentioned in the book you are what you eat. Everything that I have been through I truly believe was needed for me to have a better understanding of life and spiritual growth. To whomever is reading this: don't take life for granted. If you are living an unhealthy life please change it now because everyone doesn't get chances to correct situations in time.

Throughout this journey I was told by my kidney specialist to go to dialysis and never return to work. I was also told by my primary doctor that I should plan for my funeral. I chose not to go to dialysis.

If it wasn't for the grace of God I wouldn't be writing this book. I took the time to pray and meditate daily and get the proper rest. I stopped living to eat, and began to eat to survive. I now eat more fresh fruits and vegetables, and I stay away from processed foods because they have lots of sodium. I eat little to no red meat. I try my best to cook at home as much as possible so I can manage how much sodium goes in my food. I mainly eat Non-GMO (Genetically Modified Organism) and organic foods. Part of my daily routine includes 30 minutes of a variety of exercises. I have increased my water intake to half the ounces of my weight. I let go of almost everything in my life that drained my positive energy. Months after all of these changes I visited my physician for more test results.

When I entered the room my doctor noticed my weight loss and he began to smile at me. As he read my test results he couldn't stop smiling and neither could I. My kidney function had returned and my percentages were up. I was no longer in need of dialysis. Also for the first time in years my blood pressure was at normal levels. My doctor was amazed and he told me that he was proud of me and to keep doing whatever I'm doing because it's working.

As I look back at my entire health experience I realized the six days between the hospitalizations when I was unable to eat or drink anything were a blessing from God. It was a fast that my body needed. If you do the research you will see that fasting can change your brain functions.

I have returned to work and I continue to maintain my healthy habits. Living a healthier lifestyle has given me more energy and a clearer mindset. Don't wait until tomorrow to change. If this is you, start now because this one precious earthly life is all you have.

I AM HEALED

WALKING IN FAITH

For additional information or to contact the author:

walkinginfaith111@gmail.com

Facebook: walkinginfaith111

Follow the Author on Instagram:
walkinginfaith111

CPSIA information can be obtained
at www.ICGtesting.com
Printed in the USA
FSHW01n0748090218